I'M GROWING UP... NOW WHAT?

SEX-ED BOOK

DONIA YOUSSEF

Copyright © 2022 by Monster Publishing Limited.

All rights reserved.

No part of this book may be reproduced, stored in a retrieval system,
or transmitted in any form or by any means, electronic, mechanical, photocopying,
recording, scanning, or otherwise, without the prior written permission of the publisher.

https://monster-productions.com

ISBN: 978-1-7398724-2-7 (Paperback)
ISBN: 978-1-7398724-3-4 (Hardcover)

Illustrated by Chuileng Muivah
Book Designed by Nonon Tech & Design

Published by Monster Publishing Limited.

*Dedicated to
my daughters Aaliyah and Tiana* ♥

OUR BODIES ARE CHANGING — WHAT NOW?

You said goodbye to your friends from school, and it was summer. Now, only a few months later, you look in the mirror and what's happened?

Some of you are taller. Some of you are bigger. Some of you have hair where you didn't before. Some of you have DEEPER voices.

Most of all, all of you feel like you're in a different body.
Is it an alien's body? Someone else's body?

No, it's your body! As we get older when we reach the age we're at, our bodies begin to develop. And what is happening is completely normal.

We are becoming bigger. We're growing and changing.
So now what?

BOYS AND GIRLS ARE DIFFERENT

Bobby has hair under his arms where he didn't before.
Maria is three inches taller than she was just two months
ago on her twelfth birthday.

There are a lot of changes happening to our bodies.
And sometimes, boys and girls share these changes.
We all grow taller and bigger.

But boys and girls are *different*. And part of *growing* up is
going through puberty.

PUBER-WHAT?

Puberty. This means our bodies start making hormones. These hormones are different for boys and girls. Boys' bodies make testosterone hormones, and girls' bodies make estrogen hormones.

These hormones make girls' and boys' bodies different.

You might've heard some words at school. Words that describe our private parts. These words might make you giggle or turn your face red! But it's important to know the *right words*. The words your parents and doctors use to describe our body parts.

OUR REPRODUCTIVE AND SEXUAL BODY PARTS (Anatomy)

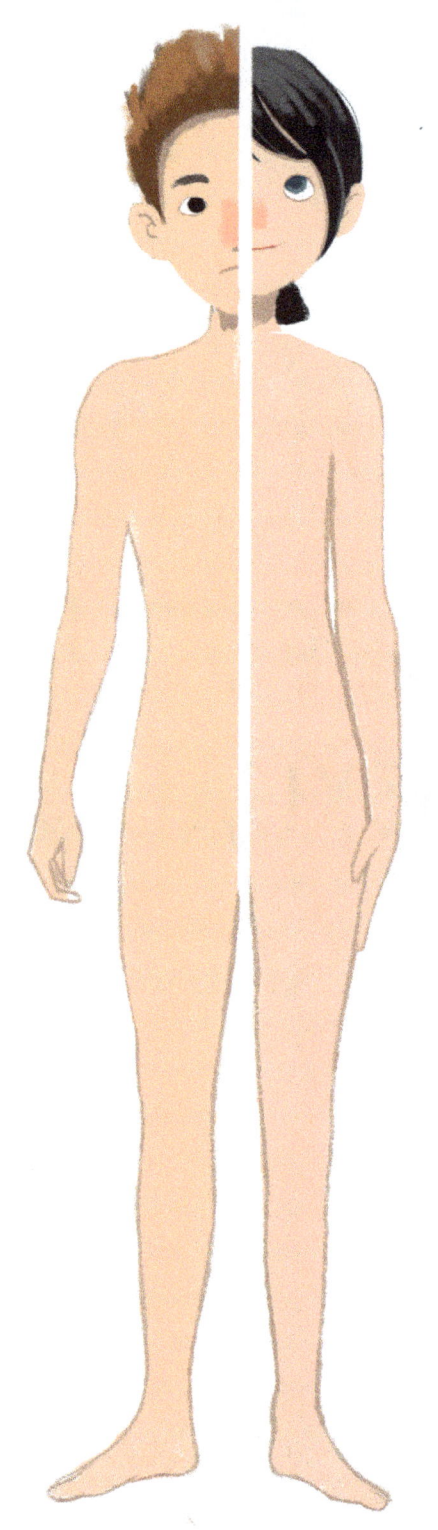

Our anatomy is our body, literally. We all have feet, toes, fingers, and eyes, and we all have ears, knees, and elbows.

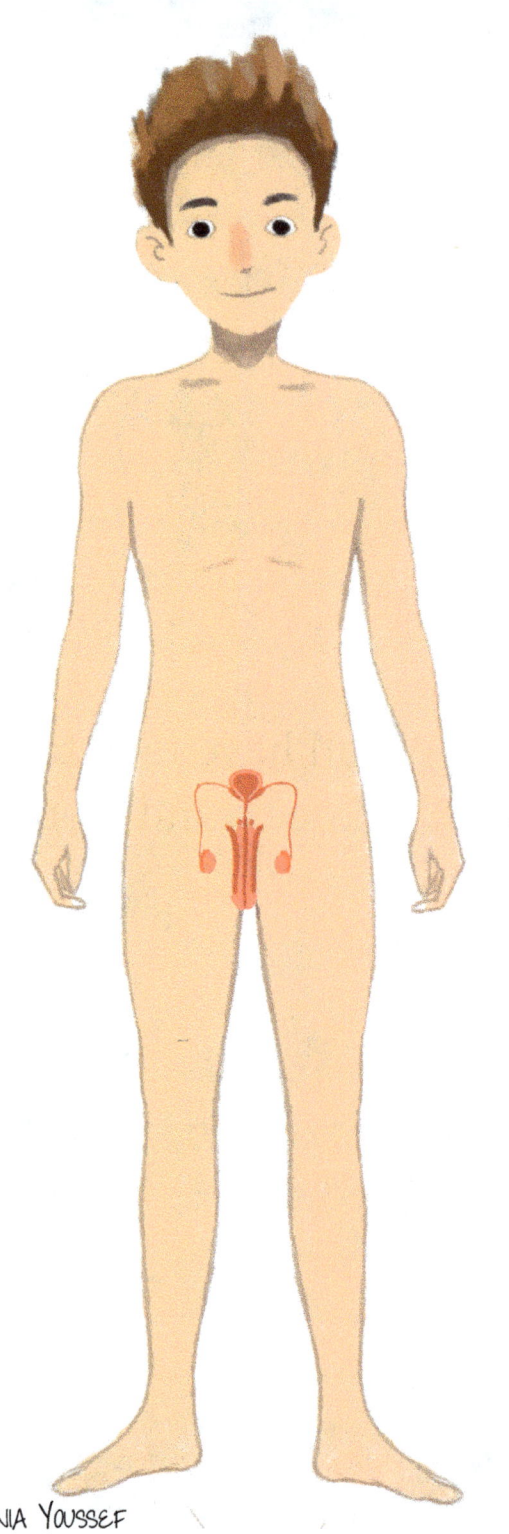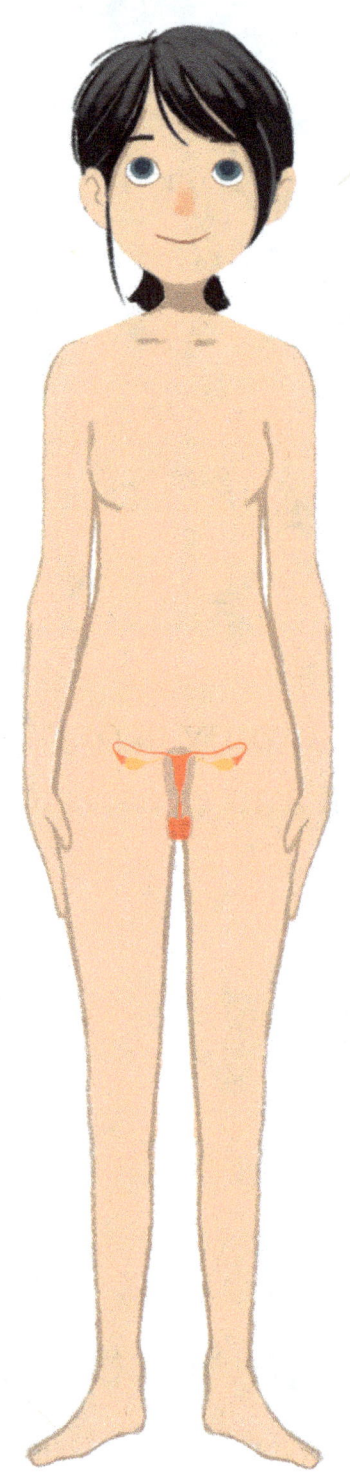

But there is a difference between boys' and girls' reproductive and sexual organs. Some of this is inside our bodies and some outside. Let's take a look at two kids going through puberty.

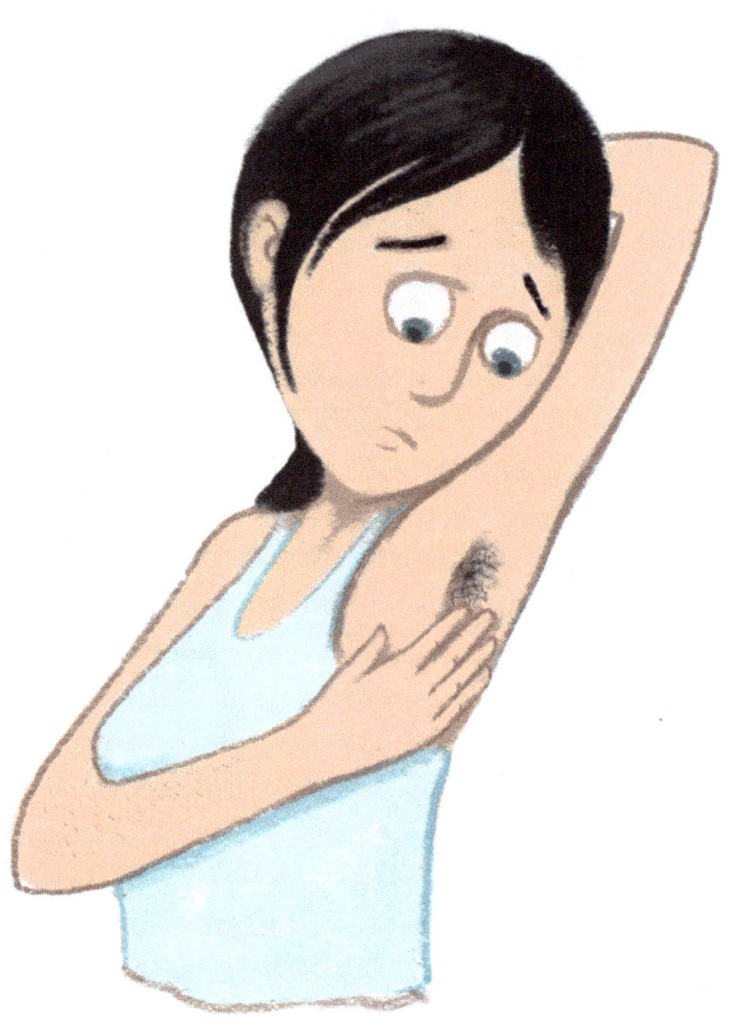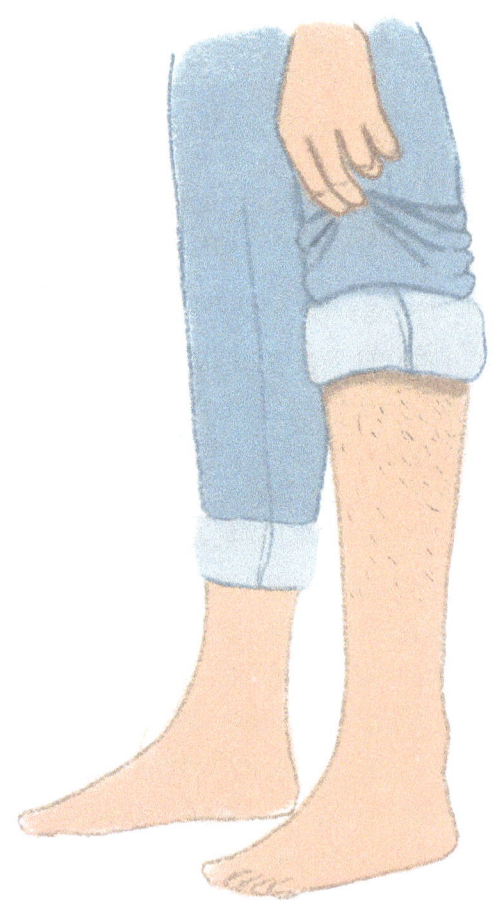

There's Maria and Noah. A girl and boy.

Maria turned thirteen, and now her body is changing. New hormones are going through her body. She has fine tiny hairs on her arms and even one or two under her armpits. And some on her legs. She even grew two inches this summer. What is going on?

Don't worry, Maria: *everything is okay*. This is all a NORMAL part of growing up.

Since Maria is a girl, she will begin to grow breasts. This is a natural part of being a girl. One day, as a woman, she may use her breasts to feed her baby.

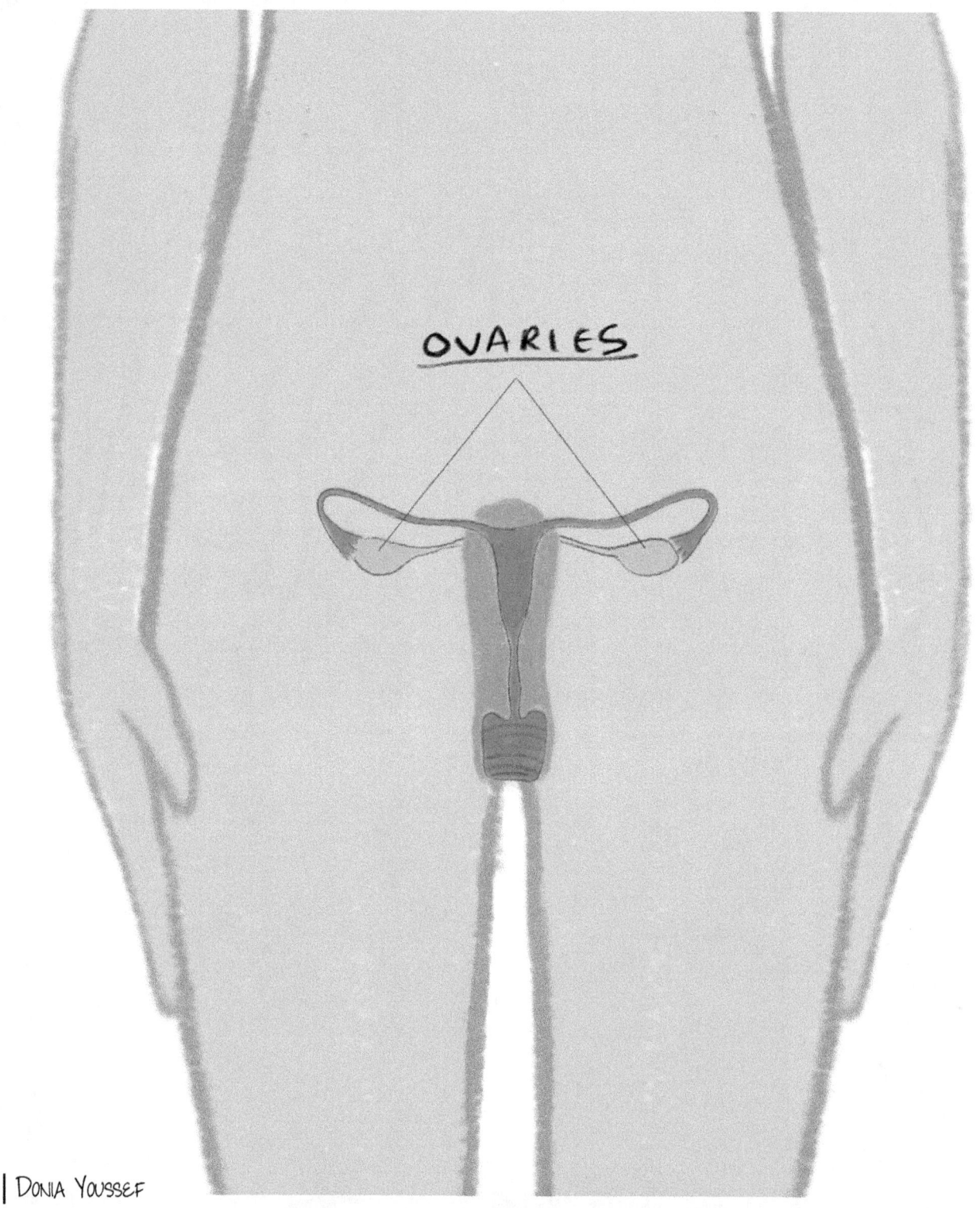

Also, since Maria is a girl, she has eggs inside her. Eggs?

Really? Yes, Maria has *ovaries*, which produce egg cells. These can become a baby one day if Maria chooses to have one as an adult. And this now brings us to Periods.

All About Periods

A period is a release of blood from a girl's uterus, out through her vagina. It is a sign that she is getting close to the end of puberty. There is a lot to learn about periods. Here are some common questions that teens have.

When Do Most Girls Get Their Period?

Most girls get their first period when they're around 12. But getting it any time between age 10 and 15 is OK. Every girl's body has its own schedule.

There isn't one right age for a girl to get her period. But there are some clues that it will start soon:

- Most of the time, a girl gets her period about 2 years after her breasts start to develop.
- Another sign is vaginal discharge fluid (sort of like mucus) that a girl might see or feel on her underwear. This discharge usually begins about 6 months to a year before a girl gets her first period.

What Causes a Period?

A period happens because of changes in hormones in the body. Hormones are chemical messengers. The ovaries release the female hormones estrogen and progesterone. These hormones cause the lining of the uterus (or womb) to build up. The built-up lining is ready for a fertilized egg to attach to and start developing. If there is no fertilized egg, the lining breaks down and bleeds. Then the same process happens all over again.

It usually takes about a month for the lining to build up, then break down. That is why most girls and women get their periods around once a month.

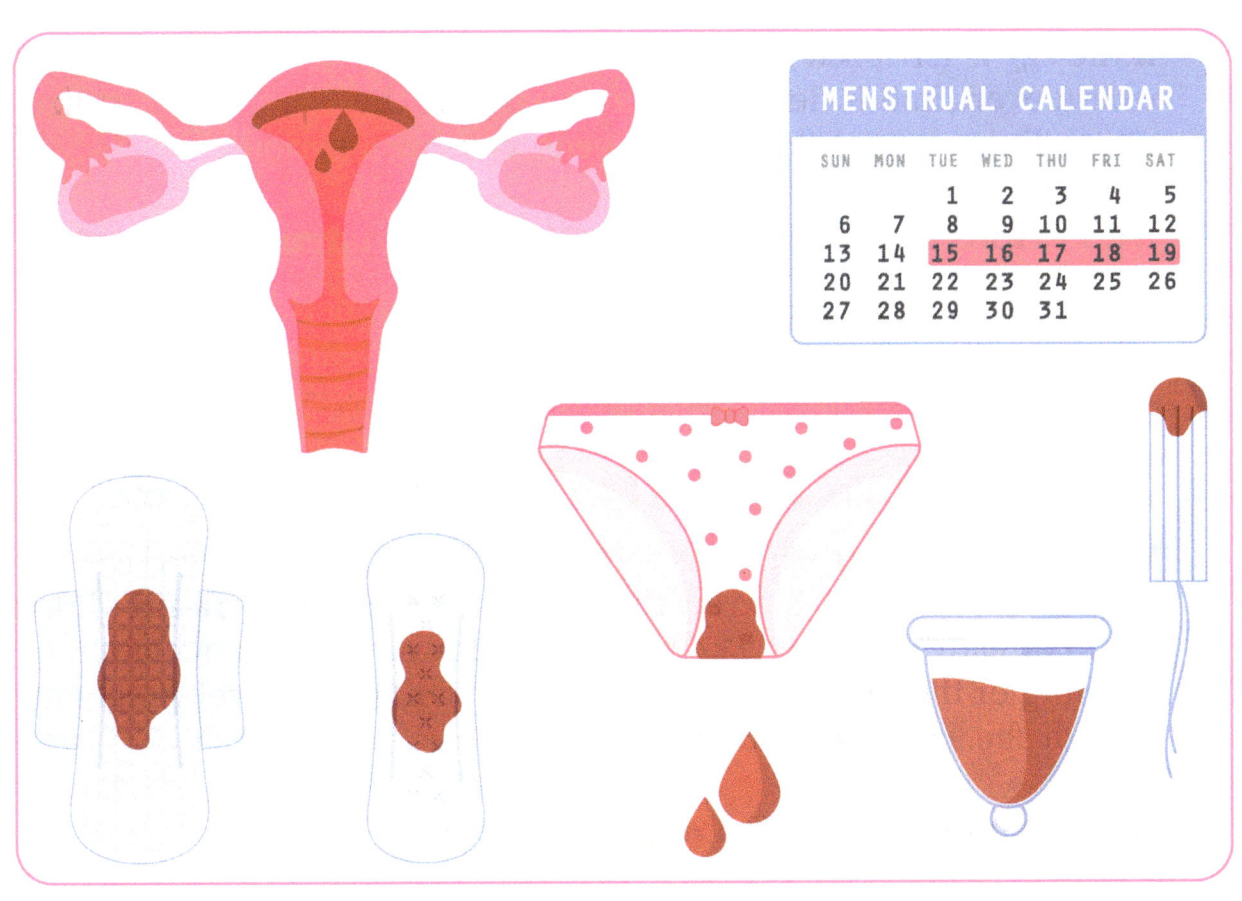

How Does Ovulation Relate to Periods?

Ovulation (pronounced: ov-yoo-LAY-shun) is the release of an egg from the ovaries. The same hormones that cause the uterus lining to build up also cause an egg to leave one of the ovaries. The egg travels through a thin tube called a fallopian tube to the uterus.

If the egg is fertilized by a sperm cell, it attaches to the wall of the uterus, where over time it develops into a baby. If the egg is not fertilized, the uterus lining breaks down and bleeds, causing a period.

Do Periods Happen Regularly When Menstruation Starts?

For the first few years after a girl starts her period, it may not come regularly. This is normal at first. By about 2–3 years after her first period, a girl's periods should be coming around once every 4–5 weeks.

Can a Girl Get Pregnant as Soon as Her Period Starts?

Yes, a girl can get pregnant as soon as her period starts. A girl can even get pregnant right before her very first period. This is because a girl's hormones might already be active. The hormones may have led to ovulation and the building of the uterine wall. If a girl has sex, she can get pregnant, even though she has never had a period.

How Long Do Periods Last?

Periods usually last about 5 days. But a period can be shorter or last longer.

How Often Does a Period Happen?

Periods usually happen about once every 4–5 weeks. But some girls get their periods a little less or more often.

Should I Use a Pad, Tampon, or Menstrual Cup?

You have many choices about how to deal with period blood. You may need to experiment a bit to find which works best for you. Some girls use only one method and others switch between different methods.

- Most girls use **pads** when they first get their period. Pads are made of cotton and come in lots of different sizes and shapes. They have sticky strips that attach to the underwear.
- Many girls find **tampons** more convenient than pads, especially when playing sports or swimming. A tampon is a cotton plug that a girl puts into her vagina. Most tampons come with an applicator that guides the tampon into place. The tampon absorbs the blood. Don't leave a tampon in for more than 8 hours because this can increase your risk of a serious infection called toxic shock syndrome.
- Some girls prefer a **menstrual cup**. Most menstrual cups are made of silicone. To use a menstrual cup, a girl inserts it into her vagina. It holds the blood until she empties it.

How Much Blood Comes Out?

It may look like a lot of blood, but a girl usually only loses a few tablespoons of blood during the whole period. Most girls need to change their pad, tampon, or menstrual cup about 3-6 times a day.

Will I Have Periods for the Rest of My Life?

When women reach menopause (around age 45-55), their periods will permanently stop. Women also won't have a period while they are pregnant.

What Is PMS?

PMS (premenstrual syndrome) is when a girl has emotional and physical symptoms that happen before or during her period. These symptoms can include moodiness, sadness, anxiety, bloating, and acne. The symptoms go away after the first few days of a period.

What Can I Do About Cramps?

Many girls have cramps with their period, especially in the first few days. If cramps bother you, you can try:

- a warm heating pad on your belly
- taking ibuprofen (Advil, Motrin, or store brand) or naproxen (Aleve or store brand)

Should I Watch for Any Problems?

Most girls don't have any problems with their periods. But call your doctor if you:

- are 15 and haven't started your period
- have had your period for more than 2 years and it still doesn't come regularly (about every 4–5 weeks)
- have bleeding between periods
- have severe cramps that don't get better with ibuprofen or naproxen
- have very heavy bleeding (bleeding that goes through a pad or tampon faster than every 1 hour)
- have periods that last more than about a week
- have severe PMS that gets in the way of your everyday activities

Looking Ahead

Periods are a natural, healthy part of a girl's life. They shouldn't get in the way of exercising, having fun, and enjoying life. If you have questions about periods, ask your doctor, a parent, health teacher, school nurse, or older sister.

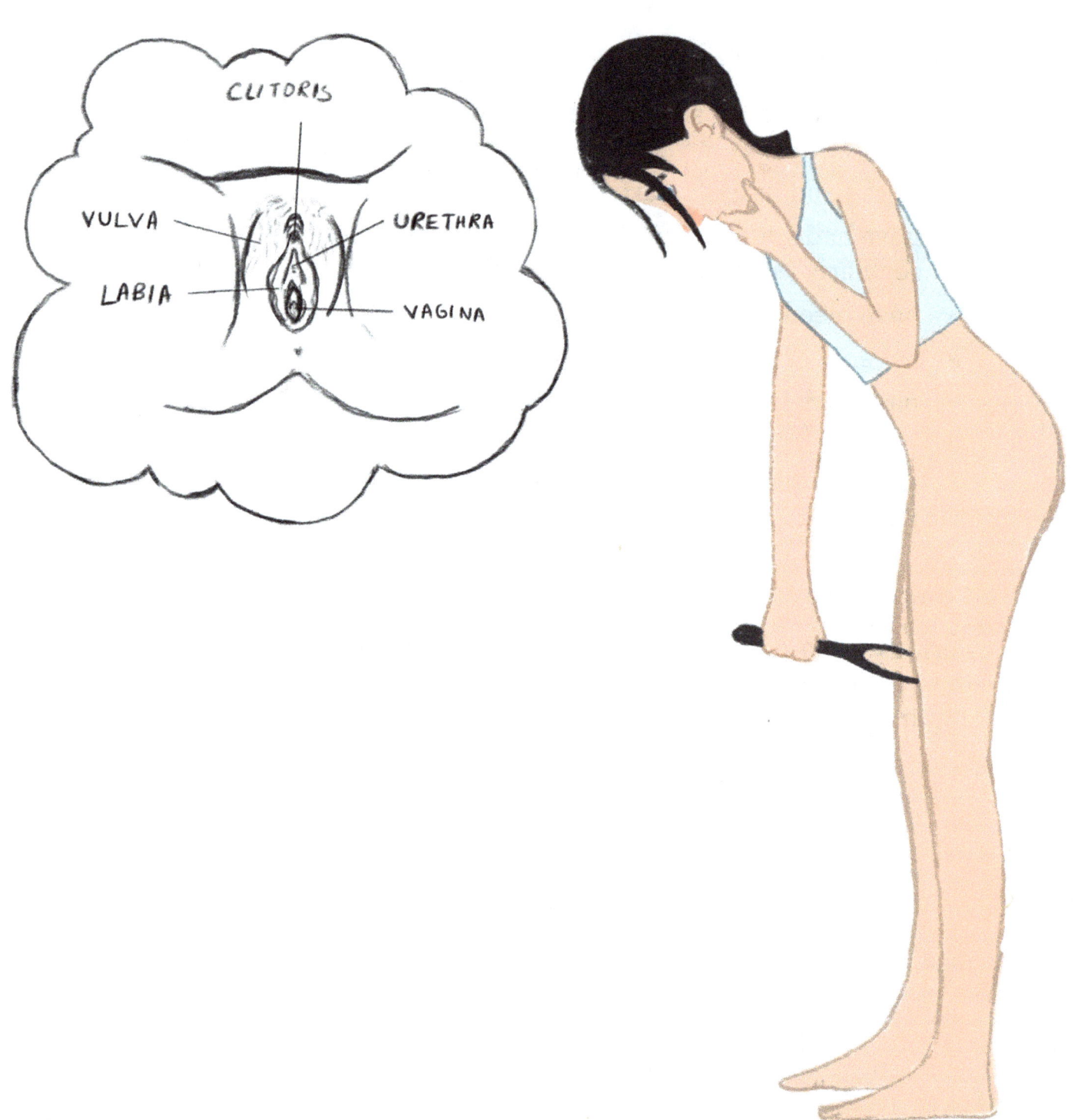

On the outside of Maria's body, she has a vagina.
This is her sexual organ. What does this mean? Don't worry,
we'll get to that!

Now, what about Noah? He's a boy, and he, too, is going through changes. He grew almost five inches! He's taller than his mum now. His voice also changed a bit. It sounds deeper, kind of like his father and big brother. He also has hair he didn't before, like on his arms and even some above his lip.

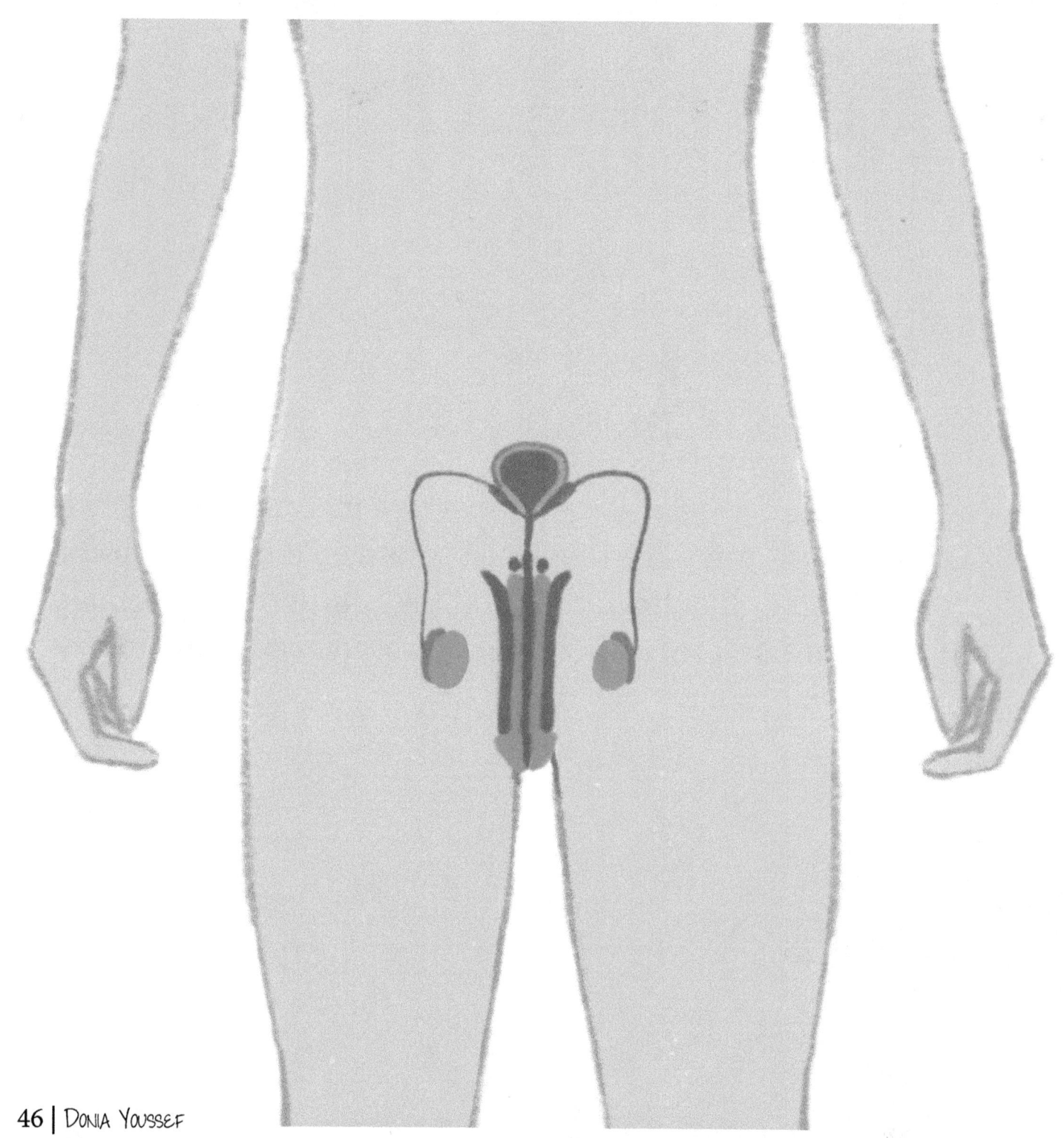

Inside Noah's body, his sexual organs are creating sperm. These are the 'seeds,' if you will, to make a baby. Male sperm can make a female's 'egg' grow into a human baby!

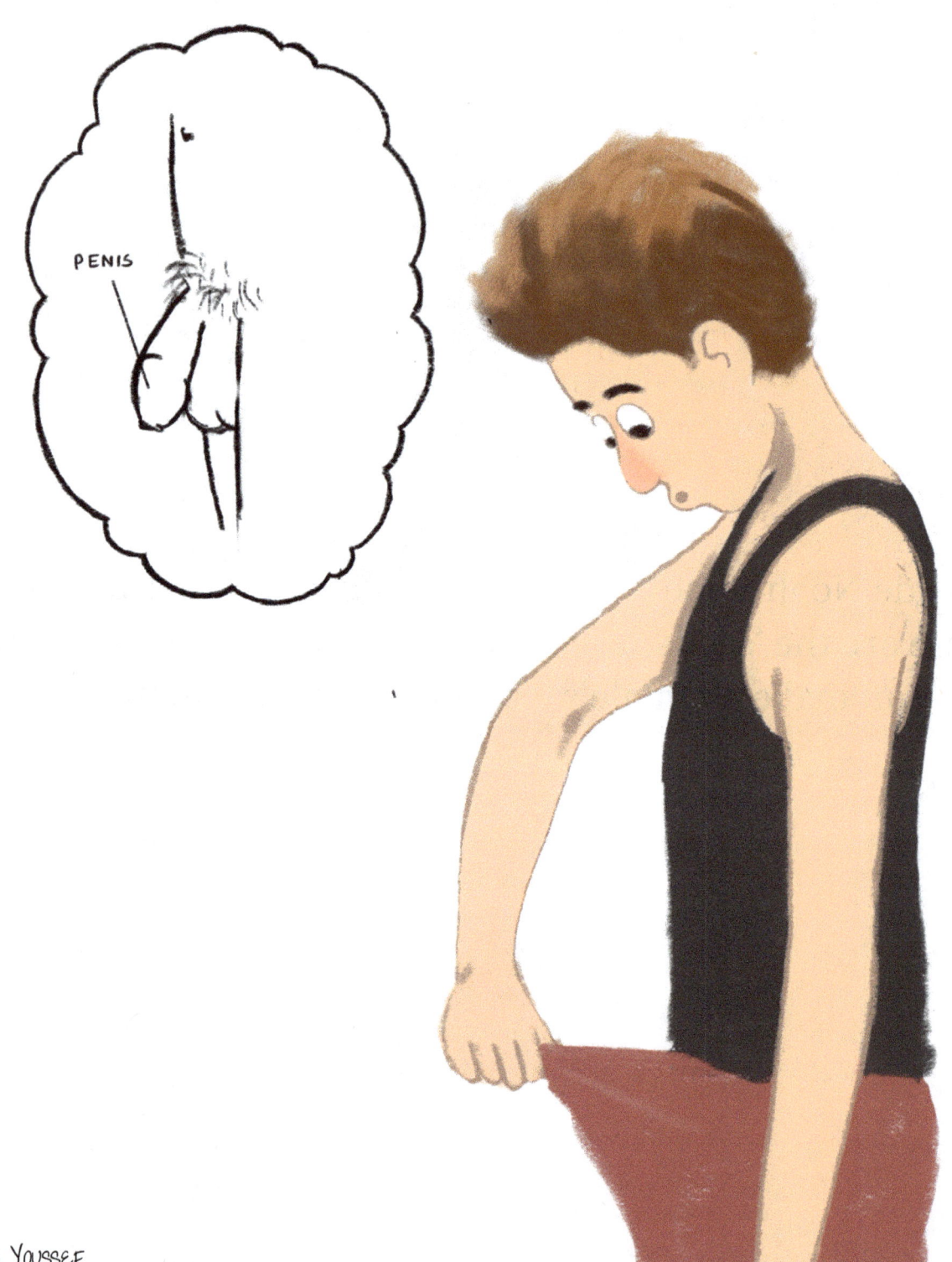

And, of course, on the outside of Noah's body, he has a penis. This is because Noah is a boy.

PRIVATE PARTS
(Being Safe)

One very important thing to remember, no matter if you are a boy or girl or whatever age you may be, your private parts ***ARE YOURS ONLY!*** That means nobody else is allowed to see, touch, or even talk about them. This is why they are called 'private parts' to begin with.

Only our parents, who may have already talked to you about these things, are allowed to discuss this. Of course, your doctor will, too. Parents, doctors, and teachers (who may be talking to you right now) are safe adults who can answer your questions about all this stuff. Just remember: *your private parts are private.*

SEX AND REPRODUCTION

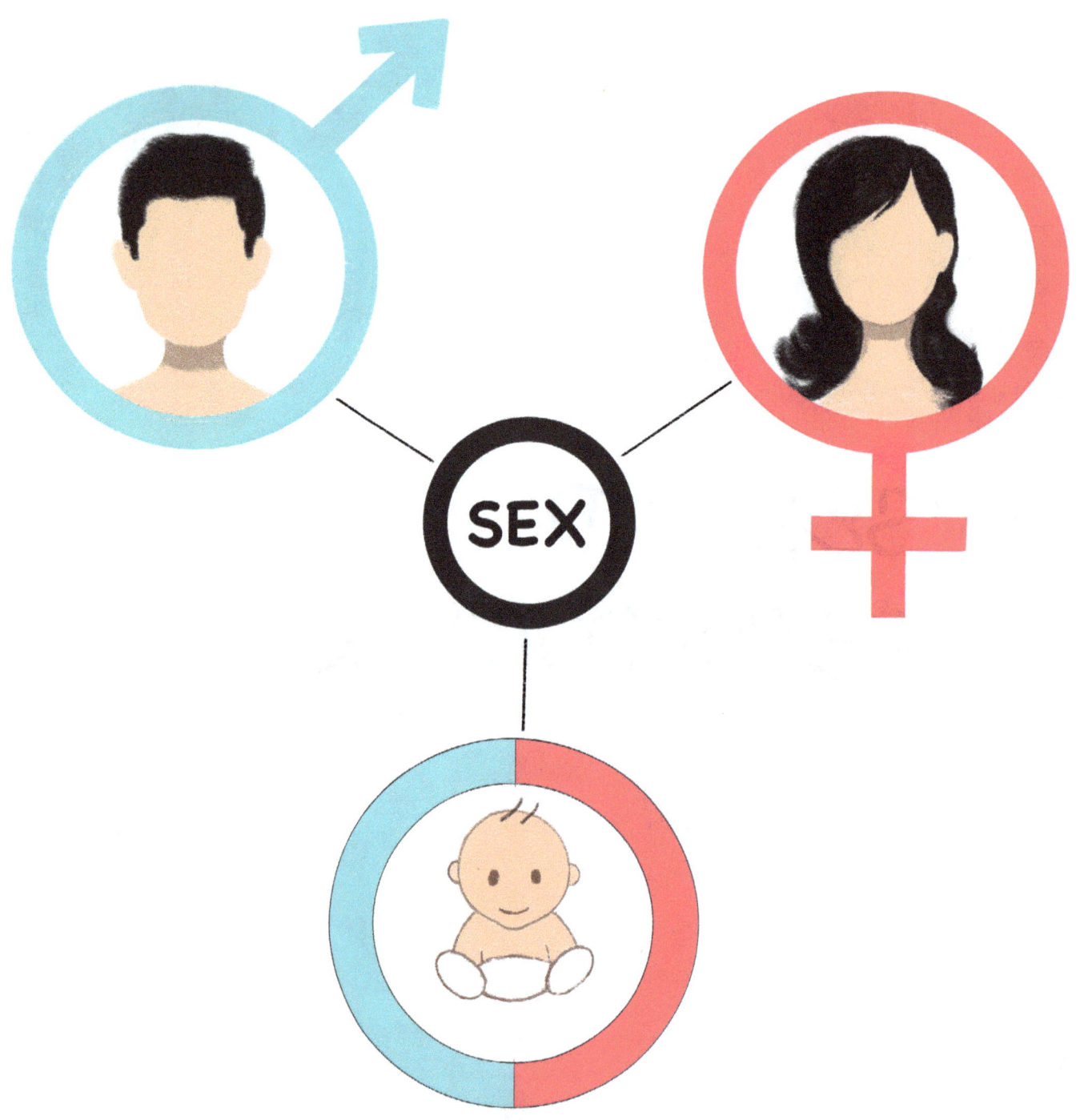

So, what is <u>sex</u>? Yes, it might make our cheeks turn red and giggle. Well, that is normal enough!

Sex is when human beings procreate: that's a fancy way of saying they make babies.

When we are adults of an age to safely engage in sexual intercourse, we experience pleasure. This bodily sense of satisfaction comes from our sexual organs: our penises and vaginas.

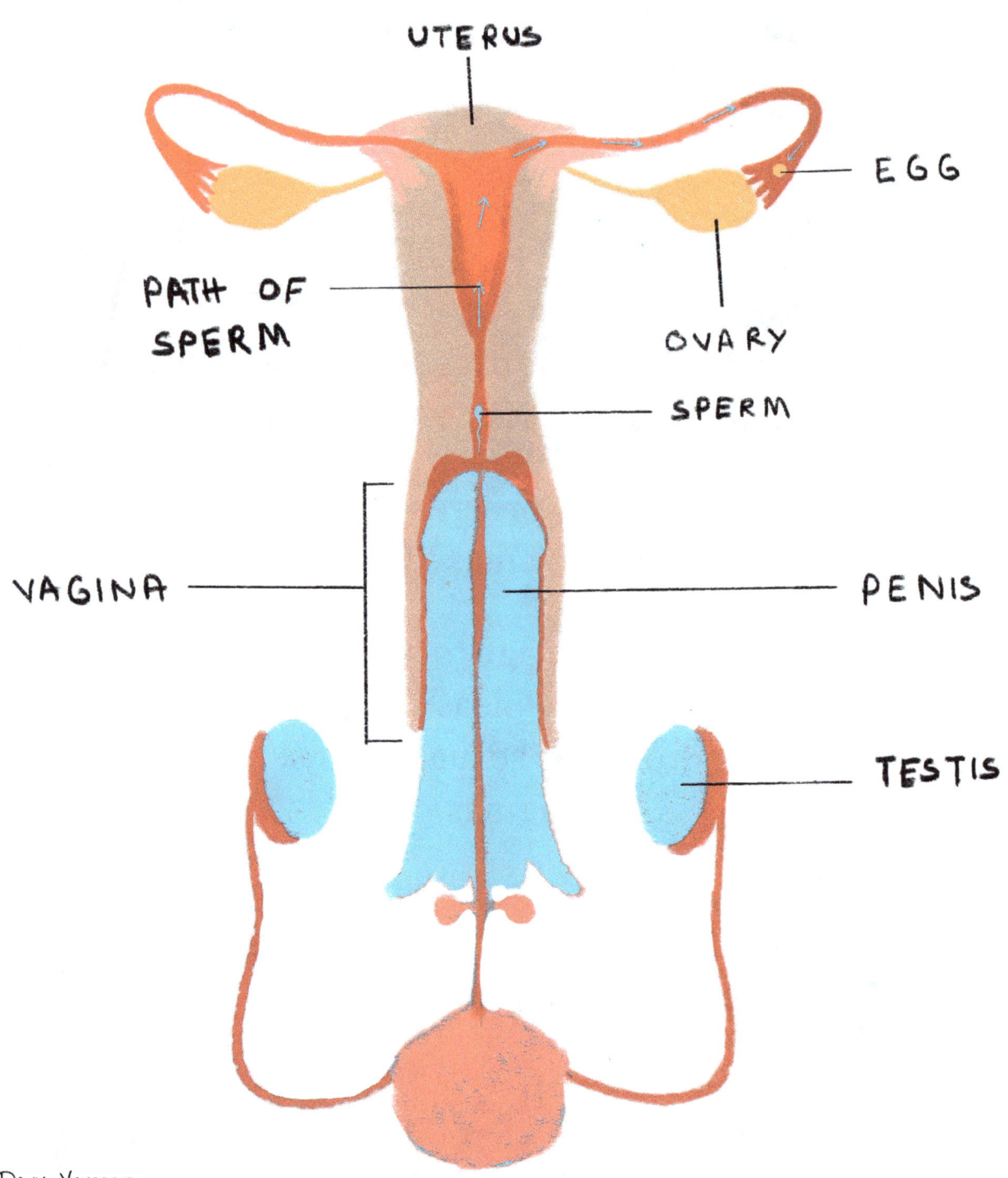

When men and women like or love each other, they will have sex. This means the man will put his penis into a woman's vagina. The sperm comes out of his penis and goes into a small tube call the fallopian tube. This is where the sperm meets the egg, and, of course, when a baby is made!

EVERYONE IS DIFFERENT-IDEAL BODY TYPES

Our bodies are unique, and everyone is different.
There is nothing to be ashamed of.

Because everyone is different, and when you look around
and see everyone changing, you might think,
'Why don't I look like her?' or 'why don't I look like him?'

Boy and girls grow up at different rates, which sometimes
means your friend might be taller or shorter than you.
This is normal. Change is going to happen—*to all of us*.

There is no ideal or perfect body type. We are all different—
and that is a good thing.

WHY DOES NOAH LOOK DIFFERENT TO ME?

Wow, what is happening when you look around? Suddenly, the boys and girls you saw before are looking different. They even make you *feel* differently.

Why is that?

When we go through puberty, the way we see others will change. Suddenly, Maria might see Noah differently. He was just a pest before always getting on her nerves.

So why does she feel differently now? Hormones are flying through her body, that's why!

She might see him as handsome (yuck!). She would never have thought that before, but now he seems strong, brave, and attractive when she looks at him!

And what about Noah? When he looked at Maria before, he only saw a girl who would chase him. And he chased her, too!

But now he thinks she is pretty. He even 'likes' her! (Uh oh!) What has happened?

———————————————————

Children, as they grow into adults, go through puberty, which not only makes their bodies change but their feelings, too.

Now kids are going to dances and going on dates. Some kids might not, and that is okay. But this is a normal part of growing up.

TV, INTERNET, AND OTHER KIDS— WHAT WE HEAR ABOUT SEX

There are many images, videos, and things we see on our televisions and the Internet that have to do with sex. Some are positive, meaning they present sex and sexual attraction in a good way. Some are negative and present sex and sexual attraction in the wrong way.

Our bodies are to be respected, whether we are a boy or girl.

Sex or sexual intercourse is something very serious. Some kids in school might say they have already done this. You don't need to take their word for it. If you have questions, ask a trusted adult: your parents or doctor.

Sex can be something beautiful, amazing, and part of a normal life, but it is something to be respected, too.

Do not ever feel pressured by someone your age to have sex. You can always go to your parents first. And, as we talked about, your private parts are private! No matter who it is, your body is yours and yours alone. Do not feel pressured to do anything, show anything, or talk about anything to someone else—even a kid your own age!

SAFE SEX

Wait, safe sex? What does that even mean? It means sex/ sexual intercourse is something to be taken very seriously. Sexually Transmitted Diseases (STDs) do exist. These are diseases that pass from one person to another during the act of sex.

This is why it's very important to learn about safe sex from trusted adults, grown ups close to us who will explain what that means. Safe sex can mean not having sex altogether to taking precautions. What is a precaution? It's when you do something to protect yourself from something. Adults will explain this to you.

ALWAYS TALK TO PARENTS-PARENTS CAN HELP-AND YOUR DOCTOR, TOO!

Do you have more questions? Well, of course!
This is a big, big topic, right?

Remember, when talking about sex and our bodies, it's important to speak to someone you trust, like your parents, doctor, or teacher who is presenting this.

Parents especially will be there for you. Our bodies and the act of sex are not something to take lightly. Ask any question you might have—there are no silly or stupid questions.
They all matter.

We are growing, changing, and that can be scary at first. *But it's all normal*. And when you learn and understand more, you will feel better!

THE END

www.ingramcontent.com/pod-product-compliance
Lightning Source LLC
Chambersburg PA
CBHW080605170426
43209CB00007B/1337